Dichotomous Keys and Mapping Codes for Wetland Landscape Position, Landform, Water Flow Path, and Waterbody Type Descriptors

Ralph W. Tiner
Regional Wetland Coordinator

U.S. Fish and Wildlife Service
National Wetlands Inventory Project
Northeast Region
300 Westgate Center Drive
Hadley, MA 01035

September 2003

Table of Contents

Section 1. Introduction

A wide variety of wetlands have formed across the United States. To describe this diversity and to inventory wetland resources, government agencies and scientists have devised various wetland classification systems (Tiner 1999). Features used to classify wetlands include vegetation, hydrology, water chemistry, origin of water, soil types, landscape position, landform (geomorphology), wetland origin, wetland size, and ecosystem form/energy sources.

The U.S. Fish and Wildlife Service's wetland and deepwater habitat classification (Cowardin et al. 1979) is the national standard for wetland classification. This classification system emphasizes vegetation, substrate, hydrology, water chemistry, and certain impacts (e.g., partly drained, excavated, impounded, and farmed). These properties are important for describing wetlands and separating them into groups for inventory and mapping purposes and for natural resource management. They do not, however, include some abiotic properties important for evaluating wetland functions (Brinson 1993). Moreover, the classification of deepwater habitats is limited mainly to general aquatic ecosystem (marine, estuarine, lacustrine, and riverine) and bottom substrate type, with a few subsystems noted for riverine deepwater habitats. The Service's classification system would benefit from the application of additional descriptors that more fully encompass the range of characteristics associated with wetlands and deepwater habitats.

In the early 1990s, Mark Brinson created a hydrogeomorphic (HGM) classification system to serve as a foundation for wetland evaluation (Brinson 1993). He described the HGM system as "a generic approach to classification and not a specific one to be used in practice" (Brinson 1993, p. 2). This system emphasized the location of a wetland in a watershed (its geomorphic setting), its sources of water, and its hydrodynamics. The system was designed for evaluating similar wetlands in a given geographic area and for developing a set of quantifiable characteristics for "reference wetlands" rather than for inventorying wetland resources (Smith et al. 1995). A series of geographically focused models or "function profiles" for various wetland types have been created and are in development for use in functional assessment (e.g., Brinson et al. 1995, Ainslie et al. 1999, Smith and Klimas 2002).

Need for New Descriptors

The Service's National Wetlands Inventory (NWI) Program has produced wetland maps for 91 percent of the coterminous United States and 35 percent of Alaska. Digital data are available for 46 percent of the former area and for 18 percent of the latter. Although these data represent a wealth of information about U.S. wetlands, they lack hydrogeomorphic and other characteristics needed to perform assessments of wetland functions over broad geographic areas. Using geographic information system (GIS) technology and geospatial databases, it is now possible to predict wetland functions for watersheds - a major natural resource planning unit. Watershed managers could make better use of NWI data if additional descriptors (e.g., hydrogeomorphic-type attributes) were added to the current NWI database. Watershed-based preliminary assessments of wetland functions could be performed. This new information would also permit more detailed characterizations of wetlands for reports and for developing scientific studies and lists of potential reference wetland sites.

Background on Development of Keys

Since the Cowardin et al. wetland classification system (1979) is the national standard and forms the basis of the most extensive wetland database for the country, it would be desirable to develop additional modifiers to enhance the current data. This would greatly increase the value of NWI digital data for natural resource planning, management, and conservation. Unfortunately, Brinson's "A Hydrogeomorphic Classification of Wetlands" (1993) was not designed for use with the Service's wetland classification. He used some terms from the Cowardin et al. system but defined them differently (e.g., Lacustrine and Riverine). Consequently, the Service needed to develop a set of hydrogeomorphic-type descriptors that would be more compatible with its system. Such descriptors would bridge the gap between these two systems, so that NWI data could be used to produce preliminary assessments of wetland functions based on characteristics identified in the NWI digital database. In addition, more descriptive information on deepwater habitats would also be beneficial. For example, identification of the extent of dammed rivers and streams in the United States is a valuable statistic, yet according to the Service's classification dammed rivers are classified as Lacustrine deepwater habitats with no provision for separating dammed rivers from dammed lacustrine waters. Differentiation of estuaries by various properties would also be useful for national or regional inventories.

Recognizing the need to better describe wetlands from the abiotic standpoint in the spirit of the HGM approach, the Service developed a set of dichotomous keys for use with NWI data (Tiner 1997b). The keys bridge the gap between the Service's wetland classification and the HGM system by providing descriptors for landscape position, landform, water flow path and waterbody type (LLWW descriptors) important for producing better characterizations of wetlands and deepwater habitats. The LLWW descriptors for wetlands can be easily correlated with the HGM types to make use of HGM profiles when they become available. The LLWW attributes were designed chiefly as descriptors for the Service's existing classification system (Cowardin et al. 1979) and to be applied to NWI digital data, but they can be used independently to describe a wetland or deepwater habitat. Consequently, there is some overlap with Cowardin et al. since some users may wish to use these descriptors without reference to Cowardin et al.

The first set of dichotomous keys was created to improve descriptions of wetlands in the northeastern United States (Tiner 1995a, b). They were initially used to enhance NWI data for predicting functions of potential wetland restoration sites in Massachusetts (Tiner 1995a, 1997a). Later, the keys were modified for use in predicting wetland functions for watersheds nationwide (Tiner 1997b, 2000). A set of keys for waterbodies was added to improve the Service's ability to characterize wetland and aquatic resources for watersheds.

The keys are periodically updated based on application in various physiographic regions. This version is an update of an earlier set of keys published in 1997 and 2000 (Tiner 1997b, 2000). Relatively minor changes have been made, including the following: 1) added "drowned river-mouth" modifier to the Fringe and Basin landforms (for use in areas where rivers empty into large lakes such as the Great Lakes where lake influences are significant), 2) added "connecting channels" to river type (to address concerns in the Great Lakes to highlight such areas), 3) added "Throughflow-intermittent" water flow path (to separate throughflow wetlands along intermittent streams from those along perennial streams), 4) added "Throughflow-artificial" and "Outflow-artificial" to water flow path (to identify former "isolated" wetlands or fragmented wetlands that are now throughflow or outflow due to ditch construction), 5) revised the lake key to focus on permanently flooded deepwater sites (note: shallow and seasonally to intermittently flooded sites are wetlands) and added "open embayment" modifier, and 6) revised the estuary type key (consolidated some types). This version also clarifies that a terrene wetland may be associated with a stream where the stream does not periodically flood the wetland. In this case, the stream has relatively little effect on the wetland's hydrology. This is especially true for numerous flatwood wetlands. It also briefly discusses how the term "isolated" is applied relative to surface water and ground water interactions. In the near future, illustrations will be added to this document to aid users in interpretations.

Use of the Keys

Two sets of dichotomous keys (composed of pairs of contrasting statements) are provided - one for wetlands and one for waterbodies. Vegetated wetlands (e.g., marshes, swamps, bogs, flatwoods, and wet meadows) and periodically exposed nonvegetated wetlands (e.g., mudflats, beaches, and other exposed shorelines) should be classified using the wetland keys, while the waterbody keys should be used for permanent deep open water habitats (subtidal or >6.6 feet deep for nontidal waters). Some sites may qualify as both wetlands and waterbodies. A good example is a pond. Shallow ponds less than 20 acres in size meet the Service's definition of wetland, but they are also waterbodies. Such areas can be classified as both wetland and waterbody, if desirable. However, we recommend that ponds be classified using the waterbody keys. Another example would be permanently flooded aquatic beds in the shallow water zone of a lake. We have classified them using wetland hydrogeomorphic descriptors, yet they also clearly represent a section of the lake (waterbody). This approach has worked well for us in producing watershed-based wetland characterizations and preliminary assessments of wetland functions.

Uses of Enhanced Digital Database

Once they are added to existing NWI digital data, the LLWW characteristics (e.g., landscape position, landform, water flow path, and waterbody type) may be used to produce a more complete description of wetland and deepwater habitat characteristics for watersheds. The enhanced NWI digital data may then be used to predict the likely functions of individual wetlands or to estimate the capacity of an entire suite of wetlands to perform certain functions in a watershed. Such work has been done for several watersheds including Maine's Casco Bay watershed and the Nanticoke River and Coastal Bays watersheds in Maryland, the Delaware portion of the Nanticoke River, and numerous small watersheds in New York (see Tiner et al. 1999, 2000, 2001; Machung and Forgione 2002; Tiner 2002; see sample reports on the NWI website:http://wetlands.fws.gov for application of the LLWW descriptors). These characterizations are based on our current knowledge of wetland functions for specific types (Tiner 2003) and may be refined in the future, as needed, based on the applicable HGM profiles and other information. The new terms can also be used to describe wetlands for reports of various kinds including wetland permit reviews, wetland trend reports, and other reports requiring more comprehensive descriptions of individual wetlands.

Organization of this Report

The report is organized into seven sections: 1) Introduction, 2) Wetland Keys, 3) Waterbody Keys, 4) Coding System for LLWW Descriptors (codes used for classifying and mapping wetlands), 5) Acknowledgments, 6) References, and 7) Glossary.

Section 2. Wetland Keys

Three keys are provided to identify wetland landscape position and landform for individual wetlands: Key A for classifying the former and Keys B and C for the latter (for inland wetlands and coastal wetlands, respectively). A fourth key - Key D - addresses the flow of water associated with wetlands. Table 1 lists the LLWW descriptors. It gives readers a good idea of what the various combinations may be. Also see wetland codes in one of the following sections.

Users should first identify the landscape position associated with the subject wetland following Key A-1. Afterwards, using Key B-1 for inland wetlands and Key C-1 for salt and brackish wetlands, users will determine the associated landform. The landform keys include provisions for identifying specific regional wetland types such as Carolina bays, pocosins, flatwoods, cypress domes, prairie potholes, playas, woodland vernal pools, West Coast vernal pools, interdunal swales, and salt flats. Key D-1 addresses water flow path descriptors. Various other modifiers may also be applied to better describe wetlands, such as headwater areas; these are included in the four main keys.

Besides the keys provided, there are numerous other attributes that can be used to describe the condition of wetlands. Some examples are other descriptors that address resource condition could be ones that emphasize human modification, (e.g., natural vs. altered, with further subdivisions of the latter descriptor possible), the condition of wetland buffers, or levels of pollution (e.g., no pollution [pristine], low pollution, moderate pollution, and high pollution). Addressing wetland condition, however, was beyond our immediate goal of describing wetlands from a hydrogeomorphic standpoint.

Table 1. List of landscape position, landform, water flow path, and waterbody type (LLWW) descriptors. Note that more detailed categorization of landforms, water flow path, and pond types are possible, but they have not been shown here.

Landscape	Landform	Water Flow Path	Waterbody Type
Marine	Fringe Island	Bidirectional-tidal	Open Ocean Reef-protected Waters Atoll Lagoon Fjord Semi-protected Oceanic Bay
Estuarine	Fringe Basin Basin (tidally restricted) Island	Bidirectional-tidal	Fjord Island Protected Rocky Headland Bay Rocky Headland Bay Tectonic Estuary River-dominated Estuary Bar-built Estuary Bar-built Estuary (Coastal Pond) Bar-built Estuary (Hypersaline Lagoon) Island-protected Estuary Shoreline Bay Estuary
Lotic	Floodplain Basin Flat Fringe Island	Throughflow Throughflow-intermittent Throughflow-entrenched Bidirectional-tidal Bidirectional-nontidal	River (Gradients: Tidal, Dammed, High, Middle, Low, and Intermittent) Stream (Gradients: Tidal, Dammed, High, Middle, Low, and Intermittent)

6

Lentic	Fringe	Bidirectional-nontidal	Natural Lake (Main Body, Open Embayment, Semi-enclosed Embayment, Barrier Beach Lagoon)
	Basin	Bidirectional-tidal	Dammed River Valley Lake (Reservoir)
	Flat	Throughflow	Dammed River Valley Lake (Hydropower)
	Island		Dammed River Valley Lake (Other)
			Other Dammed Lake (Former Natural Lake)
			Other Dammed Lake (Artificial)
Terrene	Fringe (pond)	Outflow	Pond (Natural, Dammed/Impounded, Excavated, Beaver, Other Artificial; many other types)
	Basin	Outflow-artificial	
	Basin (former floodplain)	Inflow	
	Flat	Throughflow	
	Flat (former floodplain)	Throughflow-artificial	
	Interfluve	Throughflow-entrenched	
	Slope	Isolated	
		Paludified	

Key A-1: Key to Wetland Landscape Position

This key allows characterization of wetlands based on their location in or along a waterbody, in a drainageway, or in isolation ("geographically isolated" - surrounded by upland).

1. Wetland is completely surrounded by upland (non-hydric soils)....................................**Terrene**
1. Wetland is not surrounded by upland but is connected to a waterbody of some kind.................2

2. Wetland is located in or along tidal salt or brackish waters (i.e., an estuary or ocean) including its periodically inundated shoreline (excluding areas formerly under tidal influence)...................3
2. Wetland is not periodically inundated by salt or brackish tides...4

3. Wetland is located in or along the ocean..**Marine**
                                                            Go to Key C-1 for coastal landform
3. Wetland is located in or along an estuary (typically a semi-enclosed basin or tidal river where fresh water mixes with sea water)..**Estuarine**
                        Go to Key E-2 for Estuary Type, then to Key C-1 for coastal landform

> <u>Note</u>: If area was formerly connected to an estuary but now is completely cut-off from tidal flow, consider as one of inland landscape positions - Terrene, Lentic, or Lotic, depending on current site characteristics. Such areas should be designated with a modifier to identify such wetlands as "<u>former estuarine wetland</u>." Lands overflowed infrequently by tides such as overwash areas on barrier islands are considered Estuarine. Tidal freshwater wetlands contiguous to salt/brackish/oligohaline tidal marshes are also considered Estuarine, whereas similar wetlands just upstream along strictly fresh tidal waters are considered Lotic.

4. Wetland is located in or along a lake or reservoir (permanent waterbody where standing water is typically much deeper than 6.6 feet at low water), including streamside wetlands in a lake basin and wetlands behind barrier islands and beaches with open access to a lake.............**Lentic**
                                                            Go to Key C-2 for Lake Type
                                                    Then *Go to Key B-1 for inland landform*

> <u>Note</u>: Lentic wetlands consist of all wetlands in a lake basin (i.e., the depression containing the lake), including lakeside wetlands intersected by streams emptying into the lake. The upstream limit of lentic wetlands is defined by the upstream influence of the lake which is usually approximated by the limits of the basin within which the lake occurs. The streamside lentic wetlands are designated as "<u>Throughflow</u>," thereby emphasizing the stream flow through these wetlands. Other lentic wetlands are typically classified as "<u>Bidirectional-nontidal</u>" since water tables rise and fall with lake levels during the year. Tidally-influenced freshwater lakes have "<u>Bidirectional-tidal</u>" flow.
>
> *Modifiers*: <u>Natural</u>, <u>Dammed River Valley</u>, <u>Other Dammed</u> - see Key C-2 for others.

4. Wetland does not occur along this type of waterbody...5

5. Wetland is located in a river or stream (including in-stream ponds), within its banks, or on its active floodplain <u>and</u> is periodically flooded by the river or stream..6

5. Wetland is not located in a river or stream or on its active floodplain...........................**Terrene**

> <u>Note</u>: These wetlands may occur: (1) on a slope or flat, or in a depression (including ponds, potholes, and playas) lacking a stream but contiguous to a river or stream, (2) on a historic (inactive) floodplain, or (3) in a landscape position crossed by a stream (e.g., an entrenched stream), but where the stream does not periodically inundate the wetland.
> *Go to Key B-1 for inland landform*

6. Wetland is the source of a river or stream but this watercourse does not extend through the wetland...**Terrene**

> *Modifiers*: May include <u>H</u>eadwater for wetlands that are sources of streams and <u>Estuarine Discharge</u> or <u>Marine Discharge</u> for wetlands whose outflow goes directly to an estuary or the ocean, respectively.

6. Wetland is located in a river or stream, within its banks, or on its active floodplain.................7

7. Wetland is associated with a river (a broad channel mapped as a polygon or 2-lined watercourse on a 1:24,000 U.S. Geological Survey topographic map) or its active floodplain........ ....**Lotic River**
> *Go to Couplet "a" below*
> *(Also see note under first couplet #3 - Lentic re: streamside wetlands in lake basins*)

7. Wetland is associated with a stream (a.linear or single-line watercourse on a 1:24,000 U.S. Geological Survey topographic map) or its active floodplain...................................**Lotic Stream**
> *Go to Couplet "a" below*
> *(Also see note under first couplet #3 - Lentic re: streamside wetlands in lake basins*)

> <u>Note</u>: Artificial drainageways (i.e., ditches) are not considered part of the Lotic classification, whereas channelized streams are part of the Lotic landscape position.

> *Modifiers*: <u>Headwater</u> (wetlands along first-order streams and possibly second-order streams and large wetlands in upper portion of watershed believed to be significant groundwater discharge sites) and <u>Channelized</u> (excavated stream course).

> a. Water flow is under tidal influence (freshwater tidal wetlands)..............**Tidal Gradient**
> *Go to Key B-1 for inland landform*
> a. Water flow is not under tidal influence (nontidal)...b

b. Water flow is dammed, yet still flowing downstream, at least seasonally.......................
....**Dammed Reach**

Go to Key B-1 for inland landform

Modifiers: <u>Lock and Dammed,</u> <u>Run-of-River Dam,</u> <u>Beaver Dam,</u> and <u>Other Dam</u> (see Waterbody Key B-2 for further information).

b. Water flow is unrestricted..c

c. Water flow is intermittent during the year...................................**Intermittent Gradient**

Go to Key B-1 for inland landform

c. Water flow is perennial (year-round)...d

d. Water flow is generally rapid due to steep gradient; typically little or no floodplain development; watercourse is generally shallow with rock, cobbles, or gravel bottoms; first- and second-order "streams" in hilly to mountainous terrain; part of Cowardin's Upper Perennial Subsystem..**High Gradient**

Go to Key B-1 for inland landform

d. Watercourse characteristics are not so; "stream" order greater than 2 in hilly to mountainous terrain..e

e. Water flow is generally slow; typically with extensive floodplain; water course shallow or deep with mud or sand bottoms; typically fifth and higher order "streams", but includes lower order streams in nearly level landscapes such as the Great Lakes Plain (former glacial lakebed) and the Coastal Plain, and ditches; the lower order streams may lack significant floodplain development); Cowardin's Lower Perennial subsystem.....................

....**Low Gradient**

Go to Key B-1 for inland landform

e. Water flow is fast to moderate; with little to some floodplain; usually third-, fourth- and higher order "streams" associated with hilly to mountainous terrain; part of Cowardin's Upper Perennial Subsystem...**Middle Gradient**

Go to Key B-1 for inland landform

Key B-1: Key to Inland Landforms

1. Wetland occurs on a noticeable slope (e.g., greater than a 2 percent slope)........**Slope Wetland**
Go to Key D-1 for water flow path

Modifiers can be applied to Slope Wetlands to designate the type of inflow or outflow as <u>Channelized Inflow or Outflow</u> (intermittent or perennial, stream or river), <u>Nonchannelized Inflow or Outflow</u> (wetland lacking stream, but connected by observable surface seepage flow), or <u>Nonchannelized-Subsurface Inflow or Outflow</u> (suspected subsurface flow from or to a neighboring wetland upslope or downslope, respectively).

1. Wetland does not occur on a distinct slope..2

2. Wetland forms an island..**Island Wetland**
(Go to Key D-1 for water flow path)

<u>Note</u>: Can designate an island formed in a delta at the mouth of a river or stream as a <u>Delta Island Wetland</u>; other islands are associated with landscape positions (e.g., lotic river island wetland, lotic stream island wetland, lentic island wetland, or terrene island pond wetland). Vegetation class and subclass from Cowardin et al. 1979 should be applied to characterize the vegetation of these wetland islands; vegetation is assumed to be rooted unless designated by a *modifier* - "<u>Floating Mat</u>" to indicate a floating island.

2. Wetland does not form an island..3

3. Wetland occurs within the banks of a river or stream or along the shores of a pond, lake, or island, or behind a barrier beach or island, <u>and</u> is <u>either</u>: (1) vegetated *and* typically permanently inundated, semipermanently flooded (including their tidal freshwater equivalents plus seasonally flooded-tidal palustrine emergent wetlands which tend to be flooded frequently by the tides) or otherwise flooded for most of the growing season, or permanently saturated due to this location <u>or</u> (2) a nonvegetated bank or shore that is temporarily or seasonally flooded .....**Fringe Wetland**
Go to Couplet "a" below for Types of Fringe Wetlands
Then *Go to Key D-1 for water flow path*
<u>Attention</u>: *Seasonally to temporarily flooded vegetated wetlands along rivers and streams (including tidal freshwater reaches) are classified as either Floodplain, Basin, or Flat landforms - see applicable categories.*

    a. Wetland forms along the shores of an upland island within a lake, pond, river, or stream...b
    a. Wetland does not form along the shores of an island..d

    b. Wetland forms behind a barrier island or beach spit along a lake..............<u>Lentic Barrier Island Fringe Wetland</u> or <u>Lentic Barrier Beach Fringe Wetland</u>
        Modifier: <u>Drowned River-mouth</u>
    b. Wetland forms along another type of island..c

c. Wetland forms along an upland island in a river or stream..................<u>Lotic River</u> <u>Island Fringe Wetland</u> or <u>Lotic Stream Island Fringe Wetland</u>

c. Wetland forms along an upland island in a lake or pond................<u>Lentic Island Fringe</u> <u>Wetland</u> or <u>Terrene Pond Island Fringe Wetland</u>

d. Wetland forms in or along a river or stream.........................<u>Lotic River Fringe Wetland</u> or <u>Lotic Stream Fringe Wetland</u>

d. Wetland forms in or along a pond or lake...e

e. Wetland forms along a pond shore...f

e. Wetland forms along a lake shore...............................<u>Lentic Fringe Wetland</u>
        Modifier: <u>Drowned River-mouth</u>

f. Wetland occurs along an in-stream pond.......................................<u>Lotic River or</u> <u>Stream</u> <u>Fringe Pond Wetland Throughflow</u>

f. Wetland occurs in another type of pond............................<u>Terrene Fringe Pond Wetland</u>

<u>Note</u>: Vegetation is assumed to be rooted unless designated by a *modifier* to indicate a floating mat (<u>Floating Mat</u>).

3. Wetland does not exist along these shores..4

4. Wetland occurs on an active floodplain (alluvial processes in effect).......................**Floodplain Wetland*** (could specify the river system, if desirable).   *Go to Key D-1 for water flow path* Sub-landforms are listed below.

a. Wetland forms along the shores of a river island...................<u>Floodplain Island Wetland</u>

a. Wetland is not along an island...b

b. Wetland forms in a depressional feature on a floodplain........<u>Floodplain Basin Wetland</u> or <u>Floodplain Oxbow Wetland</u> (a special type of depression)

b. Wetland forms on a broad nearly level terrace..........................<u>Floodplain Flat Wetland</u>

*<u>Note</u>: Questionable floodplain areas may be verified by consulting soil surveys and locating the presence of alluvial soils, e.g., Fluvaquents or Fluvents, or soils with Fluvaquentic subgroups. While most Floodplain wetlands will have a Throughflow water flow path; others may be designated, e.g., Inflow, Outflow, or Isolated. Former floodplain wetlands are classified as Basins or Flats and designated as former floodplain.

Modifiers: <u>Partly Drained</u>; <u>Confluence wetland</u> - wetland at the intersection of two or more streams; <u>River-mouth</u> or <u>stream-mouth wetland</u> - wetland at point where a river and stream empties into lake; <u>Meander scar wetland</u> - floodplain basin wetland, the remnant of a former river meander.

4. Wetland does not occur on an active floodplain..5

5. Wetland occurs on an interstream divide (interfluve)..................................**Interfluve Wetland** or specify *regional types* of interfluve wetlands, for example: *Carolina Bay Interfluve Wetland, Pocosin Interfluve Wetland*, and *Flatwood Interfluve Wetland* (Southeast). Sub-landforms are listed below.   *Go to Key D-1 for water flow path*

      a. Wetland forms in a depressional feature................................. Interfluve Basin Wetland
      a. Wetland forms on a broad nearly level terrace ....Interfluve Flat Wetland

      Modifiers: Partly Drained.

5. Wetland does not occur on an interfluve..6

6. Wetland exists in a distinct depression in various positions on the landscape (i.e., surrounded by upland, along smaller rivers and streams, along in-stream ponds, along lake shores, or on former floodplains or interfluves)............ **Basin Wetland** or **Basin Wetland Former Floodplain** (including *Basin Oxbow Wetland Former Floodplain*) or **Basin Wetland Former Interfluve**. Can specify regional types: *Carolina Bay Basin Wetland* and *Pocosin Basin Wetland* (Atlantic Coastal Plain), *Cypress Dome Basin Wetland* (Florida), *Prairie Pothole Basin Wetland* (Upper Midwest), *"Salt Flat" Basin Wetland* (arid West), *Playa Basin Wetland* (Southwest), *West Coast Vernal Pool Basin Wetland* (California and Pacific Northwest), *Interdunal Basin Wetland* (sand dunes), *Woodland Vernal Pool Basin Wetland* (forests throughout the country), *Polygonal Basin Wetland* (Alaska), *Sinkhole Basin Wetland* (karst/limestone regions), *Pond Wetland Basin* (throughout country), or some type of *Island Basin Wetland* for basin wetlands on islands.
                                                                   Go to Key D-1 for water flow path

      Modifiers may be applied to indicate artificially created basins due to beaver activity or human actions or artificially drained basins including: Beaver (beaver-created); wetlands created for various purposes or unintentionally formed due to human activities - may want to specify purpose like Aquaculture (e.g., fish and crayfish), Wildlife management (e.g., waterfowl impoundments), and Former floodplain, or to designate former salt marsh that is now nontidal (Former estuarine wetland). Other *modifiers* may be applied to designate the type of inflow or outflow as Channelized (intermittent or perennial, stream or river), Nonchannelized-wetland (contiguous wetland lacking stream), or Nonchannelized-subsurface flow (suspected subsurface flow to neighboring wetland), or to identify a headwater basin (Headwater) or a drainage divide wetland that discharges into two or more watershed (Drainage divide), or to denote a spring-fed wetland (Spring-fed), a wetland bordering a pond (Pond basin wetland) and a wetland bordering an upland island in a pond (Pond island border). For lotic basin wetlands, consider additional modifiers such as Confluence wetland - wetland at the intersection of two or more streams; River-mouth or Stream-mouth wetland - wetland at point where a river and a stream empties into a lake. For lentic basins associated with the Great Lakes, possibly identify Drowned River-mouth wetlands where mouth extends into the lake basin. Partly drained may be used for ditched/drained wetlands.

6. Wetland exists in a relatively level area...**Flat Wetland**
or specify *regional types* of flat wetlands, for example: **Salt Flat Wetland** (in the Great Basin) or flats that are fragments of once-larger interfluve flats or former floodplains: **Flat Wetland, Former Interfluve** or **Flat Wetland, Former Floodplain**.

Go to Key D-1 for water flow path

Note: If desirable, a *modifier* for drained flats can be applied (Partly drained). Other modifiers can be applied to designate the type of inflow or outflow as Channelized (intermittent or perennial, stream or river), Nonchannelized-wetland (contiguous wetland lacking stream), or Nonchannelized-subsurface flow (suspected subsurface flow to neighboring wetland). For lotic flat wetlands, consider additional modifiers such as confluence wetland - wetland at the intersection of two or more streams; river-mouth or stream-mouth wetland - wetland at point where a river and a stream empties into a lake.

Key C-1: Key to Coastal Landforms

1. Wetland forms a distinct island in an inlet, river, or embayment........................**Island Wetland**

Go to Key D-1 for water flow path

     a. Occurs in a delta...Delta Island Wetland
          (Could identify flood delta and ebb delta islands for tidal inlets if desirable.)
     a. Occurs elsewhere either in a river or an embayment ....b

     b. Occurs in a river..River Island Wetland
     b. Occurs in a coastal embayment..Bay Island Wetland

1. Wetland does not form such an island, but occurs behind barrier islands and beaches, or along the shores embayments, rivers, streams, and islands...2

2. Wetland occurs along the shore, contiguous with the estuarine waterbody.......**Fringe Wetland**

Go to Key D-1 for water flow path

     a. Occurs behind a barrier island or barrier beach spit..........Barrier Island Fringe Wetland
     or Barrier Beach Fringe Wetland [*Modifier* for overwash areas: Overwash]
     a. Occurs elsewhere...b

     b. Occurs along a coastal embayment or along an island in a bay.........Bay Fringe
     Wetland or Bay Island Fringe Wetland or Coastal Pond Fringe Wetland (a special type of embayment, typically with periodic connection to the ocean unless artificially connected by a bulkheaded inlet) or Coastal Pond Island Fringe Wetland
     b. Occurs elsewhere...c

c. Occurs along a coastal river or along an island in a river...............River Fringe Wetland or River Island Fringe Wetland

c. Occurs elsewhere..d

d. Occurs along an oceanic island...Ocean Island Fringe Wetland

d. Occurs along the shores of exposed rocky mainland...............Headland Fringe Wetland

2. Wetland is separated from main body of marsh by natural or artificial means; the former may be connected by a tidal stream extending through the upland or by washover channels (e.g., estuarine intertidal swales), whereas the latter occurs in an artificial impoundment or behind a road or railroad embankment where tidal flow is at least somewhat restricted........**Basin Wetland**
Go to Key D-1 for water flow path

Modifiers may be applied to separate natural from created basins (managed fish and wildlife areas; aquaculture impoundments; salt hay diked lands; tidally restricted-road, and tidally restricted-railroad), and for other situations, as needed.

Key D-1: Key to Water Flow Paths

1. Wetland is periodically flooded by tides......................................**Bidirectional-tidal**
See Key F-2 for additional descriptors based on tidal ranges (i.e., macrotidal, mesotidal, and microtidal).

1. Wetland is not flooded by tides...2

2. Water levels fluctuate due to lake influences or to variable river levels, but water does not flow through this wetland...**Bidirectional-nontidal**

Note: Lentic wetlands with streams running through them are classified as Throughflow to emphasize this additional water source, while lentic wetlands located in coves or fringing the high ground would typically be classified as Bidirectional-Nontidal. Similarly, many floodplain wetlands are throughflow types, while some are connected to the river through a single channel in which water rises and falls with changing river levels. The water flow path of the latter types is best classified as bidirectional-nontidal.

2. Wetland is not subject to lake influences..3

3. Wetland is formed by paludification processes where in areas of low evapotranspiration and high rainfall, peat moss moves uphill creating wetlands on hillslopes (i.e., wetland develops upslope of primary water source)...**Paludified**

3. Wetland is not formed by paludification processes..4

4. Wetland receives surface or ground water from a stream, other waterbody or wetland (i.e., at a higher elevation) and surface or ground water passes through the subject wetland to a stream, another wetland, or other waterbody at a lower elevation; a flow-through

system....**Throughflow**, **Throughflow-intermittent***, **Throughflow-entrenched***, or **Throughflow-artificial***

> *Modifiers*: <u>Groundwater-dominated</u> throughflow wetlands can be separated from <u>Surface water-dominated</u> throughflow wetlands.
>
> <u>*Note</u>: **Throughflow-intermittent** is to be used with throughflow wetlands along intermittent streams; **Throughflow-entrenched** indicates that stream flow is through a wetland but the stream is deeply cut and does not overflow into the wetland (therefore the stream is, for practical purposes, separate from the wetland) - this water flow path is intended to be used with Terrene wetlands in this situation; **Throughflow-artificial** is used to designate wetlands where throughflow is human-caused - usually to indicate connection of Terrene wetlands to other Terrene wetlands and waters by ditches and not by streams either natural or channelized

4. Water does not pass through this wetland to other wetlands or waters.....................................5

5. There is no surface or groundwater inflow from a stream, other waterbody, or wetland (i.e., no documented surface or ground water inflow from a wetland or other waterbody at a higher elevation) <u>and</u> no observable or known outflow of surface or ground water to other wetlands or waters..**Isolated**

<u>Attention</u>: *In most applications, isolation is interpreted as "geographically isolated" since groundwater connections are typically unknown for specific wetlands. For practical purposes then," isolated" means no obvious surface water connection to other wetlands and waters. If hydrologic data exist for a locale that documents groundwater linkages, such wetlands should be identified as either outflow. inflow, or throughflow with a "<u>Groundwater-dominated</u>" modifier and not be identified as isolated <u>unless</u> the whole network of wetlands is not connected to a stream or river. In the latter case, the network is a collection of interconnected isolated wetlands.*

5. Wetland is not hydrologically or geographically isolated..6

6. Wetland receives surface or ground water inflow from a wetland or other waterbody (perennial or intermittent) at a higher elevation <u>and</u> there is no observable or known significant outflow of surface or ground water to a stream, wetland or waterbody at a lower elevation
....**Inflow**

> *Modifiers*: <u>Groundwater-dominated</u> inflow wetlands can be separated from <u>Surface water-dominated</u> inflow wetlands; <u>Human-caused</u> (usually to indicate connection of Terrene wetlands to other Terrene wetlands and waters [e.g., Inflow human-caused] by ditches and not by streams either natural or channelized).

6. Wetland receives no surface or ground water inflow from a wetland or permanent waterbody at a higher elevation (may receive flow from intermittent streams only) <u>and</u> surface or ground

water is discharged from this wetland to a stream, wetland, or other waterbody at a lower elevation..**Outflow** or **Outflow-artificial***

> *Modifiers:* <u>Groundwater-dominated</u> outflow wetlands can be separated from <u>Surface water-dominated</u> outflow wetlands. Might consider separating perennial outflow (**Outflow-perennial**) from intermitttent outflow (**Outflow-intermittent**), if interested.

> *<u>Note</u>: Outflow-artificial is usually used to indicate outflow from formerly isolated wetlands resulting by ditches.

Section 3. Waterbody Keys

These keys are designed to expand the classification of waterbodies beyond the system and subsystem levels in the Service's wetland classification system (Cowardin et al. 1979). Users are advised first to classify the waterbody in one of the five ecosystems: 1) marine (open ocean and associated coastline), 2) estuarine (mixing zone of fresh and ocean-derived salt water), 3) lacustrine (lakes, reservoirs, large impoundments, and dammed rivers), 4) riverine (undammed rivers and tributaries), and 5) palustrine (e.g., nontidal ponds) and then apply the waterbody type descriptors below.

Five sets of keys are given. Key A-2 helps describe the major waterbody type. Key B-2 identifies different stream gradients for rivers and streams. It is similar to the subsystems of Cowardin's Riverine system, but includes provisions for dammed rivers to be identified as well as a middle gradient reach similar to that of Brinson's hydrogeomorphic classification system. The third key, Key C-2, addresses lake types, while Keys D-2 and E-2 further define ocean and estuary types, respectively. Key F-2 is a key to water flow paths of waterbodies. Key G-2 is for describing general circulation patterns in estuaries. The coastal terminology applies concepts of coastal hydrogeomorphology.

Besides the keys provided, there are numerous other attributes that can be used to describe the condition of waterbodies. Some examples are other descriptors that address resource condition could be ones that emphasize human modification, (e.g., natural vs. altered, with further subdivisions of the latter descriptor possible), the condition of waterbody buffers (e.g., stream corridors), or levels of pollution (e.g., no pollution [pristine], low pollution, moderate pollution, and high pollution).

Key A-2. Key to Major Waterbody Type

1. Waterbody is predominantly flowing water..2
1. Waterbody is predominantly standing water...7

> Note: Fresh waterbodies may be tidal; if so, waterbody is classified as a <u>Tidal Lake</u> or <u>Tidal Pond</u> using criteria below to separate lakes from ponds.

2. Flow is unidirectional and waterbody is a river, stream, or similar channel..............................3
2. Flow is tidal (bidirectional) at least seasonally; waterbody is an ocean, embayment, river, stream, or lake..4

3. Waterbody is a polygonal feature on a U.S. Geological Survey map or a National Wetlands Inventory Map (1:24,000/1:25,000)..**River**
3. Waterbody is a linear feature on such maps..**Stream**
> *Go to River/Stream Gradient Key - Key B-2 - for other modifiers*

4. Waterbody is freshwater...5
4. Waterbody is salt or brackish...6

5. Waterbody is a polygonal feature on a U.S. Geological Survey map or a National Wetlands Inventory Map (1:24,000/1:25,000)..**River**
5. Waterbody is a linear feature on such maps..**Stream**
> *Go to River/Stream Gradient Key - Key B-2 - for other modifiers*

6. Part of a major ocean or its associated embayment (Marine system of Cowardin et al. 1979) ....**Ocean**
> *Go to Ocean Key - Key D-2*

6. Part of an estuary where fresh water mixes with salt water (Estuarine system of Cowardin et al. 1979)...**Estuary**
> *Go to Estuary Key - Key E-2*

7. Waterbody is freshwater...8
7. Waterbody is salt or brackish and tidal..10

8. Waterbody is permanently flooded and deep (>than 6.6 ft at low water), excluding small "kettle or bog ponds" (i.e., usually less than 5 acres in size and surrounded by bog vegetation)..**Lake**
> *Go to Lake Key - Key C-2*

8. Waterbody is shallow (< 6.6 ft at low water) or a small "kettle or bog pond" (with deeper water)..9

9. Waterbody is small (< 20 acres)..**Pond**

> Separate <u>natural</u> from <u>artificial</u> ponds, then add other modifiers like the following. Some *examples* of modifiers for ponds: <u>beaver, alligator, marsh, swamp, vernal, Prairie Pothole, Sandhill, sinkhole/karst, Grady, interdunal, farm-cropland, farm-livestock, golf, industrial, sewage/wastewater treatment, stormwater, aquaculture-catfish, aquaculture-shrimp, aquaculture-crayfish, cranberry, irrigation, aesthetic-business, acid-mine, arctic polygonal, kettle, bog, woodland, borrow pit, Carolina bay, tundra, coastal plain, tidal,</u> and <u>in-stream</u>.

> <u>Note</u>: Wetlands associated with ponds are typically either Terrene basin wetlands, such as a Cypress dome or cypress-gum pond, or Terrene pond fringe wetlands, such as semipermanently flooded wetlands along margins of pond. In-stream ponds are in the Lotic landscape position.

9. Waterbody is large (≥20 acres)..**Lake**
> *Go to Lake Key - Key C-2*

10. Part of a major ocean or its associated embayment (Marine system of Cowardin et al. 1979) ....**Ocean**
> *Go to Ocean Key - Key D-2*

10. Part of an estuary where fresh water mixes with salt water (Estuarine system of Cowardin et al. 1979)..**Estuary**
> *Go to Estuary Key - Key E-2*

Key B-2. River/Stream Gradient and Other Modifiers Key

Please note that the river/stream gradient extends from the freshwater tidal zone through the intermittent reach. The limits of the latter are typically defined by drainageways with well-defined channels that discharge water seasonally. From a practical standpoint, the limits of the lotic system are displayed on 1:24,000 U.S. Geological Survey topographic maps or similar digital data. Intermittent streams, certain dammed portions of rivers plus lock and dammed canal systems may be classified as rivers using the descriptors presented in these keys. In the Cowardin et al. system, they may be classified as Riverine Intermittent Streambed or Lacustrine Unconsolidated Bottom, respectively.

1. Water flow is under tidal influence..**Tidal Gradient**

> *Type of tidal river or stream*: 1) <u>natural river</u>, 2) <u>natural stream</u>, 3) <u>channelized river</u>, 4) <u>channelized stream</u>, 5) <u>canal</u> (artificial polygonal lotic feature), 6) <u>ditch</u> (artificial linear lotic feature), 7) <u>restored river segment</u> (part of river where restoration was performed), and 8) <u>restored stream segment</u> (part of stream where restoration was performed).

1. Water flow is not under tidal influence (nontidal)..2

2. Water flow is dammed, yet still flowing downstream at least seasonally..........**Dammed Reach**

> *Type of dammed river*: 1) <u>lock and dammed</u> (canalized river, a series of locks and dams are present to aid navigation), 2) <u>run-of-river dammed</u> (low dam allowing flow during high water periods; often used for low-head hydropower generation), and 3) <u>other dammed</u> (unspecified, but not major western hydropower dam as such waterbodies are considered lakes, e.g., Lake Mead and Lake Powell).

2. Water flow is unrestricted...3

3. Water flow is perennial (year-round); perennial rivers and streams........................4
3. Water flow is seasonal or aperiodic (intermittent); Cowardin's Intermittent Subsystem ....
....**Intermittent Gradient***

4. Water flow is generally rapid due to steep gradient; typically little or no floodplain development; watercourse is generally shallow with rock, cobbles, or gravel bottoms; first and second order "streams"; part of Cowardin's Upper Perennial subsystem...............**High Gradient***
4. Water flow is not so; some to much floodplain development..................................5

5. Water flow is generally slow; typically with extensive floodplain; water course shallow or deep with mud or sand bottoms; typically fifth and higher order "streams", but includes lower order streams in nearly level landscapes such as the Great Lakes Plain (former glacial lakebed) and the Coastal Plain (the latter streams may lack significant floodplain development); Cowardin's Lower Perennial subsystem ....**Low Gradient***
5. Water flow is fast to moderate; with little to some floodplain; usually third and fourth order "streams"; part of Cowardin's Upper Perennial subsystem...............................**Middle Gradient***

*Type of river or stream - additional modifiers that may be applied as desired: 1) <u>natural river-single thread</u> (one channel), 2) <u>natural river-multiple thread (braided)</u> (multiple, wide, shallow channels), 3) <u>natural river-multiple thread (anastomosed)</u> (multiple, deep narrow channels), 4) <u>natural stream-single thread</u>, 5) <u>channelized river</u> (dredged/excavated), 6) <u>channelized stream</u>, 7) <u>canal</u> (artificial polygonal lotic feature), 8) <u>ditch</u> (artificial linear lotic feature), 9) <u>restored river segment</u> (part of river where restoration was performed), 10) <u>restored stream segment</u> (part of stream where restoration was performed), and 11) <u>connecting channel</u> (joins two lakes). Other possible descriptors: 1) for perennial rivers and streams - <u>riffles</u> (shallow, rippling water areas), <u>pools</u> (deeper, quiet water areas), and <u>waterfalls</u> (cascades), 2) for water depth of perennial rivers - <u>deep rivers</u> ($\geq$6.6 ft at low water) from <u>shallow rivers</u> (<6.6 ft at low water), 3) nontidal river or stream segment emptying into an estuary, ocean, or lake (<u>estuary-discharge</u>, <u>marine-discharge</u>, or <u>lake-discharge</u>), 4) classification by stream order (1st, 2nd, 3rd, etc. for perennial segments), and 5) channels patterns (<u>straight</u>, <u>slight meandering</u>, <u>moderate meandering</u>, and <u>high meandering</u>).

Key C-2. Key to Lakes.

The lake designation is for permanently flooded deep waters (>6.6 feet). Some classification systems include shallow waterbodies or periodically exposed areas as "lakes." The Cowardin et al. system considers standing waterbodies larger than 20 acres to be part of the lacustrine system (regardless of water depth; shallow = wetlands; >6.6 feet = deepwater habitat), and smaller ones typically part of the palustrine wetlands. For our purposes, "shallow lakes" and "seasonal or intermittent lakes" are considered some type of terrene or lotic wetland depending on the presence and location of a stream. Lentic wetlands are associated with permanently flooded standing waterbodies deeper than 6.6 feet at low water.

1. Waterbody is not dammed or impounded..**Natural Lake**

> *Modifiers*: <u>Main body</u>, <u>Open embayment</u>, <u>Semi-enclosed embayment</u>, <u>Barrier beach lagoon</u>, <u>Seiche-influenced</u>, <u>River-fed</u> and <u>Stream-fed</u> descriptors. Can also use applicable modifiers listed under Pond (see Key A-2).

> *Can use additional modifiers listed under Pond (see Key A-2) and others (e.g., crater, lava flow, aeolian, fjord, oxbow, other floodplain, glacial, alkali, and manmade), as appropriate.

1. Waterbody is dammed, impounded, or excavated 2

2. Waterbody is dammed or impounded..3
2. Waterbody is excavated..**Excavated Lake**

3. Dammed river valley..**Dammed River Valley Lake**

> *Modifiers*: <u>Reservoir</u>, <u>Hydropower</u>, and <u>Seiche-influenced</u>; also <u>River-fed</u> and <u>Stream-fed</u> descriptors.

> <u>Note</u>: When the dam inundates former floodplains and other low-lying areas, the waterbody is considered a Dammed River Valley Lake. If the dam crosses a higher gradient river and increase water depth in an channel without significant flooding of much neighboring "land," the waterbody is considered the dammed reach of a river.

3. Dammed natural lake or other landscape..**Other Dammed Lake**

> *Modifiers*: <u>Former natural lake</u>, <u>Artificial lake</u>, <u>River-fed</u> and <u>Stream-fed</u> descriptors.

Key D-2. Key to Oceans and Marine Embayments.

1. Waterbody is completely open, not protected by any feature.................................**Open Ocean**
     (Can further identify <u>open bays</u> if desirable.)
1. Waterbody is somewhat protected...2

2. Associated with coral reef or island 3

2. Not associated with coral reef or island...4

3. Open but protected by coral reef ....**Reef-protected Waters**
3. Protected by a coral island...**Atoll Lagoon**

4. Deep embayment cut by glaciers, with an underwater sill at front end, restricting circulation;
associated with rocky headlands...**Fjord**
4. Other semi-protected embayment..**Semi-protected Oceanic Bay**

     Modifiers for all types above: <u>Submerged vegetation</u> (e.g., eelgrass or turtle-grass) or
     <u>Floating vegetation</u> (e.g., macroalgae such as kelp beds).

Key E-2. Key to Estuaries.

The following types should encompass most of the estuaries located in the United States. There
may be estuaries that do not fit within this classification. Such types should be brought to the
attention of the author.

1. Estuary is surrounded by rocky headlands and shores...2
1. Estuary is not surrounded by rocky headlands and shores..4

2. Deep embayment cut by glaciers, with an underwater sill at front end, restricting circulation
(e.g., Puget Sound)...**Fjord Estuary**
2. Not so, either open or semi-enclosed..3

3. Protected by islands....................................**Island Protected Rocky Headland Bay Estuary**
3. Not protected by islands...**Rocky Headland Bay Estuary**

     Modifiers: <u>Open</u> or <u>Semi-enclosed</u>

4. Estuary is tectonically formed (e.g., San Franciso Bay), including volcanic activity.................
....**Tectonic Estuary**

     Modifiers: <u>Fault-formed</u> and <u>Volcanic-formed</u>

4. Estuary is not tectonically formed or is formed by volcanic activity.....................................5

5. Estuary is river-dominated with a delta formed at the mouth of the river where it enters the sea (e.g., Mississippi River Delta)..**River-dominated Estuary**

5. Estuary is not river-dominated...6

6. Estuary is a drowned river valley (e.g., Chesapeake Bay)........**Drowned River Valley Estuary**

    Modifiers: Open Bay, River Channel, and Semi-enclosed Bay

6. Estuary is not a drowned river valley...7

7. Estuary formed behind and is protected by sandy barrier islands or barrier beaches (spits)...**Bar-built Estuary**

    Modifiers: Coastal Pond (oligohaline to saline) and Hypersaline Lagoon (hypersaline)

7. Estuary is not behind sandy barrier islands or beaches...8

8. Estuary is protected by reefs or other islands....................................**Island Protected Estuary**

8. Estuary is an open or semi-enclosed embayment....................................**Shoreline Bay Estuary**

Modifiers for all estuarine waterbodies: Inlet (includes any ebb- or flood- deltas that are completed submerged), Stabilized Inlet, Shoal (shallow water area), Submerged vegetation (e.g., eelgrass or turtle-grass) or Floating vegetation (e.g., macroalgae such as kelp beds).

Key F-2. Key to Water Flow Paths

1. Water flow is tidally influenced..2
1. Water flow is not under the influence of the tides..4

2. Tide range is greater than 4m (approx. >12 feet) ....**Macrotidal**
2. Tidal range is less than 4m 3

3. Tidal range is 2-4m (approx. 6-12 feet) ....**Mesotidal**
3. Tidal range is less than 2m (approx. < 6 feet) ....**Microtidal**

4. Water flows out of the waterbody via a river, stream, or ditch, with little or no inflow (inflow could be from intermittent streams or ground water only) ....**Outflow**

> *Modifier*: Human-caused for inflow via a ditch network. Might consider separating perennial outflow (**Outflow-perennial**) from intermitttent outflow (**Outflow-intermittent**), if interested.

4. Water flow is not so..5

5. Water enters waterbody from river, stream, or ditch, flows through it, and continues to flow downstream..**Throughflow** or **Throughflow-intermittent**

> *Modifier*: Human-caused for throughflow via a ditch network
>
> Note: Throughflow intermittent is applied to intermittent streams

5. Water flow is not throughflow..6

6. Water flows in and out of the waterbody through the same channel; it does not flow through the waterbody..**Bidirectional-nontidal**

6. Water flow is not bidirectional...7

7. Water flow enters via a river, stream, or ditch, but does not exit pond, lake or reservoir; waterbody serves as a sink for water..**Inflow**

> *Modifier*: Human-caused for inflow via a ditch network.

7. No apparent channelized inflow, source of water either by precipitation or by underground sources..**Isolated**

<u>Attention</u>: *In most applications, isolation is interpreted as "geographically isolated" since groundwater connections are typically unknown for specific waterbodies. For practical purposes then," isolated" means no obvious surface water connection to other wetlands and*

waters. If hydrologic data exist for a locale that document groundwater linkages, such waterbodies should be identified as either outflow. inflow, or throughflow <u>with a "Groundwater-dominated" modifier added</u> and not be identified as isolated <u>unless</u> the whole network of waterbodies is not connected to a stream or river. In the latter case, the network is a collection of interconnected isolated waterbodies.

Key G-2. Key to Estuarine Hydrologic Circulation Types

1. Estuary is river-dominated with distinct salt wedge moving seasonally up and down the river; fresh water at surface with most saline waters at bottom; low energy system with silt and clay bottoms ....**Salt-wedge Estuary**
1. Estuary is not river-dominated 2

2. Estuarine water is well-mixed, no significant salinity stratification, salinity more or less the same from top to bottom of water column; high-energy system with sand bottom...............
....**Homogeneous Estuary**
2. Estuarine water is partially mixed, salinities different from top to bottom, but not strongly stratified; low energy system ....**Partially Mixed Estuary**

Section 4. Coding System for LLWW Descriptors

The following is the coding scheme for expanding classification of wetlands and waterbodies beyond typical NWI classifications. When enhancing NWI maps/digits, codes should be applied to all mapped wetlands and deepwater habitats (including linears). At a minimum, landscape position (including lotic gradient), landform, and water flow path should be applied to wetlands, and waterbody type and water flow path to water to waterbodies. Wetland and deepwater habitat data for specific estuaries, lakes, and river systems could be added to existing digital data through use of geographic information system (GIS) technology.

Codes for Wetlands

Wetlands are typically classified by landscape position, landform, and water flow path. Landforms are grouped according to Inland types and Coastal types with the latter referring to tidal wetlands associated with marine and estuarine waters. Use of other descriptors tends to be optional. They would be used for more detailed investigations and characterizations.

Landscape Position

ES	Estuarine
LE	Lentic
LR	Lotic river
LS	Lotic stream
MA	Marine
TE	Terrene

Lotic Gradient

1	Low	
2	Middle	
3	High	
4	Intermittent	
5	Tidal	
6	Dammed	
a		lock and dammed
b		run-of-river dam
c		beaver
d		other dammed
7	Artificial (ditch)	

Lentic Type

1		Natural deep lake (see also Pond codes for possible specific types)
a		main body
b		open embayment
c		semi-enclosed embayment
d		barrier beach lagoon
2		Dammed river valley lake
a		reservoir
b		hydropower
c		other
3		Other dammed lake
a		former natural
b		artificial
4		Excavated lake
a		quarry lake
5		Other artificial lake

Estuary Type

1		Drowned river valley estuary
a		open bay (fully exposed)
b		semi-enclosed bay
c		river channel
2		Bar-built estuary
a		coastal pond-open
b		coastal pond-seasonally closed
c		coastal pond-intermittently open
d		hypersaline lagoon
3		River-dominated estuary
4		Rocky headland bay estuary
a		island protected
5		Island protected estuary
6		Shoreline bay estuary
a		open (fully exposed)
b		semi-enclosed
7		Tectonic
a		fault-formed
b		volcanic-formed
8		Fjord
9		Other

Inland Landform

SL	Slope	
SLpa		Slope, paludified
IL	Island*	
ILde		Island, delta
ILrs		Island, reservoir
ILpd		Island, pond
FR	Fringe*	
FRil		Fringe, island*
FRbl		Fringe, barrier island
FRbb		Fringe, barrier beach
FRpd		Fringe, pond
FRdm		Fringe, drowned river mouth
FP	Floodplain	
FPba		Floodplain, basin
FPox		Floodplain, oxbow
FPfl		Floodplain, flat
FPil		Floodplain, island
IF	Interfluve	
IFba		Interfluve, basin
IFfl		Interfluve, flat
BA	Basin	
BAcb		Basin, Carolina bay
BApo		Basin, pocosin
BAcd		Basin, cypress dome
BApp		Basin, prairie pothole
BApl		Basin, playa
BAwc		Basin, West Coast vernal pool
BAid		Basin, interdunal
BAwv		Basin, woodland vernal
BApg		Basin, polygonal
BAsh		Basin, sinkhole
BApd		Basin, pond
BAgp		Basin, grady pond
BAsa		Basin, salt flat
BAaq		Basin, aquaculture (created)
BAcr		Basin, cranberry bog (created)
BAwm		Basin, wildlife management (created)
BAip		Basin, impoundment (created)

BAfe	Basin, former estuarine wetland
BAff	Basin, former floodplain
BAfi	Basin, former interfluve
BAfo	Basin, former floodplain oxbow
BAdm	Basin, drowned river-mouth

FL	Flat	
FLsa		Flat, salt flat
FLff		Flat, former floodplain
FLfi		Flat, former interfluve

*Note: Inland slope wetlands and island wetlands associated with rivers, streams, and lakes are designated as such by the landscape position classification (e.g., lotic river, lotic stream, or lentic), therefore no additional terms are needed here to convey this association.

Coastal Landform

IL	Island	
ILdt		Island, delta
ILde		Island, ebb-delta
ILdf		Island, flood-delta
ILrv		Island, river
ILst		Island, stream
ILby		Island, bay

DE	Delta	
DEr		Delta, river-dominated
DEt		Delta, tide-dominated
DEw		Delta, wave-dominated

FR	Fringe	
FRal		Fringe, atoll lagoon
FRbl		Fringe, barrier island
FRbb		Fringe, barrier beach
FRby		Fringe, bay
FRbi		Fringe, bay island
FRcp		Fringe, coastal pond
FRci		Fringe, coastal pond island
FRhl		Fringe, headland
FRoi		Fringe, oceanic island
FRlg		Fringe, lagoon
FRrv		Fringe, river
FRri		Fringe, river island
FRst		Fringe, stream

FRsi   Fringe, stream island

BA   Basin
  BAaq   Basin, aquaculture (created)
  BAid   Basin, interdunal (swale)
  BAst   Basin, stream
  BAsh   Basin, salt hay production (created)
  BAtd   Basin, tidally restricted/road (not a management area)
  BAtr   Basin, tidally restricted/railroad (not a management area)
  BAwm   Basin, wildlife management (created)
  BAip   Basin, impoundment (created)

Water Flow Path

  PA   Paludified
  IS   Isolated
  IN   Inflow
  OU   Outflow
  OA   Outflow-artificial*
  OP   Outflow-perennial
  OI   Outflow-intermittent
  TH   Throughflow
  TA   Throughflow - artificial*
  TN   Throughflow - entrenched
  TI   Throughflow - intermittent
  BI   Bidirectional Flow - nontidal
  BT   Bidirectional Flow - tidal

*Note: To be used with wetlands connected to streams by ditches.

Other Modifiers (apply at the end of the code as appropriate)

  br   barren
  bv   beaver
  ch   channelized flow
  cl   coastal island (wetland on an island in an estuary or ocean including barrier islands)
  cr   cranberry bog
  dd   drainage divide
  dr   partly drained
  ed   freshwater wetland discharging directly into an estuary
  fe   former estuarine wetland
  fg   fragmented
  fm   floating mat
  gd   groundwater-dominated (apply to Water Flow Path only)

31

hi	severely human-induced		
hw	headwater		
li	lake island (wetland associated with a lake island)		
md	freshwater wetland discharging directly into marine waters		
ow	overwash		
pi	pond island border		
ri	river island (wetland associated with a river island)		
sd	surface water-dominated (apply to Water Flow Path only)		
sf	spring-fed		
ss	subsurface flow		
td	tidally restricted/road		
tr	tidally restricted/railroad		

(Note: "ho" was formerly used to indicate human-induced outflow brought about by ditch construction; now this is addressed by the water flow path "OA" Outflow-Artificial.)

Codes for Waterbodies (Deepwater Habitats and Ponds)

Besides Waterbody Type, waterbodies can be classified by water flow path (for lakes and ponds), estuary hydrologic type (for estuaries), and tidal range types (for estuaries and oceans).

Waterbody Type

RV	River		
	1	low gradient	
	a		connecting channel
	b		canal
	2	middle gradient	
	a		connecting channel
	3	high gradient	
	a		waterfall
	b		riffle
	c		pool
	4	intermittent gradient	
	5	tidal gradient	
	6	dammed gradient	
	a		lock and dammed
	b		run-of-river dammed
	c		other dammed
ST	Stream		
	1	low gradient	
	a		connecting channel
	2	middle gradient	
	a		connecting channel

3	high gradient	
a		waterfall
b		riffle
c		pool
4	intermittent gradient	
5	tidal gradient	
6	dammed	
a		lock and dammed
b		run-of-river dammed
c		beaver dammed
d		other dammed
7	artificial	
a		connecting channel
b		ditch

LK   Lake

1	natural lake (*see also Pond codes for possible specific types*)	
a		main body
b		open empbayment
c		semi-enclosed embayment
d		barrier beach lagoon
2	dammed river valley lake	
a		reservoir
b		hydropower
c		other
3	other dammed lake	
a		former natural
b		artificial
4	other artificial lake	

(Consider using a modifier to highlight specific lakes as needed, especially the Great Lakes, e.g., LK1E for Lake Erie or LK2O for Lake Ontario, and Lake Champlain, LK1C)

EY   Estuary

1	drowned river valley estuary	
a		open bay (fully exposed)
b		semi-enclosed bay
c		river channel
2	bar-built estuary	
a		coastal pond-open
b		coastal pond-seasonally closed
c		coastal pond-intermittently open
d		hypersaline lagoon
3	river-dominated estuary	

4	rocky headland bay estuary	
a		island protected
5	island protected estuary	
6	shoreline bay estuary	
a		open (fully exposed)
b		semi-enclosed
7	tectonic	
a		fault-formed
b		volcanic-formed
8	fjord	
9	other	

<u>Note</u>: If desired, you can also designate river channel (rc), stream channel (sc),and inlet channel (ic) by modifiers. *Examples*: EY1rc = Drowned River Valley Estuary river channel; EY2ic= Bar-built estuary inlet channel. If not, simply classify all estuarine water as a single type, e.g., EY1 for Drowned River Valley or EY2 for Bar-built Estuary.

OB	Ocean or Bay	
	1	open (fully exposed)
	2	semi-protected oceanic bay
	3	atoll lagoon
	4	other reef-protected waters
	5	fjord

PD	Pond		
	1	natural	
	a		bog
	b		woodland-wetland
	c		woodland-dryland
	d		prairie-wetland (pothole)
	e		prairie-dryland (pothole)
	f		playa
	g		polygonal
	h		sinkhole-woodland
	i		sinkhole-prairie
	j		Carolina bay
	k		pocosin
	l		cypress dome
	m		vernal-woodland
	n		vernal-West Coast
	o		interdunal
	p		grady
	q		floodplain
	r		other

2	dammed/impounded
a	agriculture
a1	cropland
a2	livestock
a3	cranberry
b	aquaculture
b1	catfish
b2	crayfish
c	commercial
c1	commercial-stormwater
d	industrial
d1	industrial-stormwater
d2	industrial-wastewater
e	residential
e1	residential-stormwater
f	sewage treatment
g	golf
h	wildlife management
i	other recreational
o	other
3	excavated
a	agriculture
a1	cropland
a2	livestock
a3	cranberry
b	aquaculture
b1	catfish
b2	crayfish
c	commercial
c1	commercial-stormwater
d	industrial
d1	industrial-stormwater
d2	industrial-wastewater
e	residential
e1	residential-stormwater
f	sewage treatment
g	golf
h	wildlife management
i	other recreational
j	mining
j1	sand/gravel
j2	coal
o	other
4	beaver
5	other artificial

Water Flow Path

IN	Inflow
OU	Outflow
OA	Outflow-artificial*
OP	Outflow-perennial
OI	Outflow-intermittent
TH	Throughflow
TA	Throughflow-artificial*
TI	Throughflow-intermittent*
TN	Throughflow-entrenched
BI	Bidirectional-nontidal
IS	Isolated
MI	Microtidal
ME	Mesotidal
MC	Macrotidal

*Note: OA and TA are human-caused by ditches; TI is to be used with throughflow ponds along intermittent streams.

Estuarine Hydrologic Circulation Type

SW	Salt-wedge/river-dominated type
PM	Partially mixed type
HO	Homogeneous/high energy type

Other Modifiers (apply at end of code)

ch	Channelized or Dredged
dv	Diverted
ed	freshwater stream flowing directly into an estuary
fv	Floating vegetation (on the surface)
lv	Leveed
md	freshwater stream flowing directly into marine waters
sv	Submerged vegetation

Section 5. Acknowledgments

The following individuals have assisted in the application of pilot studies which helped improve this classification: Herbert Bergquist, Gabriel DeAlessio, Bobbi Jo McClain, Glenn Smith, Matthew Starr, and John Swords. Others providing input into the refinement of this classification included Dennis Peters, Norm Mangrum, Greg Pipkin, Charlie Storrs, and Eileen Blok. Doug Wilcox provided information on the classification of Great Lakes coastal wetlands. Their contributions have made the system suitable for operational use.

Section 6. References

Ainslie, W.B., R.D. Smith, B.A. Pruitt, T.H. Roberts, E.J. Sparks, L. West, G.L. Godshalk, and M.V. Miller. 1999. A Regional Guidebook for Assessing the Functions of Low Gradient, Riverine Wetlands in Western Kentucky. U.S. Army Engineer Waterways Experiment Station, Vicksburg, MS. Technical Report WRP-DE-17.

Brinson, M.M. 1993. A Hydrogeomorphic Classification for Wetlands. U.S. Army Corps of Engineers, Washington, DC. Wetlands Research Program, Technical Report WRP-DE-4.

Brinson, M.M., F.R. Hauer, L.C. Lee, W.L. Nutter, R.D. Rheinhardt, R.D. Smith, and D. Whigham. 1995. A Guidebook for Application of Hydrogeomorphic Assessments to Riverine Wetlands. U.S. Army Engineer Waterways Experiment Station, Vicksburg, MS. Technical Report WPR-DE-11.

Cowardin, L.M., V. Carter, F.C. Golet, and E.T. LaRoe. 1979. Classification of Wetlands and Deepwater Habitats of the United States. U.S. Fish and Wildlife Service, Washington, DC. FWS/OBS-79/31.

Machung, L. and H.M. Forgione. 2002. A landscape level approach to wetland functional assessment for the New York City water supply watersheds. In: R.W. Tiner (compiler). Watershed-based Wetland Planning and Evaluation. A Collection of Papers from the Wetland Millennium Event (August 6-12, 2000; Quebec City, Quebec, Canada). Distributed by the Association of State Wetland Managers, Inc., Berne, NY. pp. 41-57.

Smith, R.D., A. Ammann, C. Bartoldus, and M.M. Brinson. 1995. An Approach for Assessing Wetland Functions Using Hydrogeomorphic Classification, Reference Wetlands, and Functional Indices. U.S. Army Engineer Waterways Experiment Station, Vicksburg, MS. Technical Report WRP-DE-9.

Smith, R.D. and C.V. Klimas. 2002. A Regional Guidebook for Applying the Hydrogeomorphic Approach to Assessing Wetland Functions of Selected Regional Wetland Subclasses, Yazoo Basin, Lower Mississippi River Alluvial Valley. U.S. Army Engineer Research and Development Center, Vicksburg, MS. Technical Report ERCD/EL TR-02-04.
Tiner, R.W. 1995a. A Landscape and Landform Classification for Northeast Wetlands

(Operational Draft). U.S. Fish and Wildlife Service, Ecological Services (NWI), Region 5, Hadley, MA.

Tiner, R.W. 1995b. Piloting a more descriptive NWI. National Wetlands Newsletter 19 (5): 14-16.

Tiner, R.W. 1997a. Adapting the NWI for preliminary assessment of wetland functions. In: The Future of Wetland Assessment: Applying Science through the Hydrogeomorphic Assessment Approach and Other Approaches. Abstracts. The Association of State Wetland Managers, Berne, NY. pp. 105-106.

Tiner, R.W. 1997b. Keys to Landscape Position and Landform Descriptors for U.S. Wetlands (Operational Draft). U.S. Fish and Wildlife Service, Northeast Region, Hadley, MA.

Tiner, R.W. 1999. Wetland Indicators: A Guide to Wetland Identification, Delineation, Classification, and Mapping. Lewis Publishers, CRC Press, Boca Raton, FL.

Tiner, R.W. 2000. Keys to Waterbody Type and Hydrogeomorphic-type Wetland Descriptors for U.S. Waters and Wetlands (Operational Draft). U.S. Fish and Wildlife Service, Northeast Region, Hadley, MA.

Tiner, R., S. Schaller, D. Petersen, K. Snider, K. Ruhlman, and J. Swords. 1999. Wetland Characterization Study and Preliminary Assessment of Wetland Functions for the Casco Bay Watershed, Southern Maine. U.S. Fish and Wildlife Service, Northeast Region. Hadley, MA. With Support from the State of Maine's Wetlands Steering Committee. Prepared for the Maine State Planning Office, Augusta, ME.

Tiner, R., M. Starr, H. Bergquist, and J. Swords. 2000. Watershed-based Wetland Characterization for Maryland's Nanticoke River and Coastal Bays Watersheds: A Preliminary Assessment Report. U.S. Fish and Wildlife Service, Northeast Region, Hadley, MA. Prepared for the Maryland Department of Natural Resources, Annapolis, MD. (see copy on the web at: http://wetlands.fws.gov listed under reports and publications)

Tiner, R.W., H.C. Bergquist, J.Q. Swords, and B.J. McClain. 2001. Watershed-based Wetland Characterization for Delaware's Nanticoke River Watershed: A Preliminary Assessment Report. U.S. Fish and Wildlife Service, Northeast Region, Hadley, MA. Prepared for the Delaware Department of Natural Resources and Environmental Control, Division of Soil and Water Conservation, Dover, DE.

Tiner, R.W. 2002. Enhancing wetland inventory data for watershed-based wetland characterizations and preliminary assessments of wetland functions. In: R.W. Tiner (compiler). Watershed-based Wetland Planning and Evaluation. A Collection of Papers from the Wetland Millennium Event (August 6-12, 2000; Quebec City, Quebec, Canada). Distributed by the Association of State Wetland Managers, Inc., Berne, NY. pp. 17-39. (http://www.aswm.org)

Tiner, R.W. 2003. Correlating Enhanced National Wetlands Inventory Data With Wetland Functions for Watershed Assessments: A Rationale for Northeastern U.S. Wetlands. U.S. Fish and Wildlife Service, National Wetlands Inventory Program, Northeast Region, Hadley, MA.

Section 7. Glossary

Barrier Beach -- a coastal peninsular landform extending from the mainland into the ocean or large embayment or large lake (e.g., Great Lakes), typically providing protection to waters on the backside and allowing the establishment of salt marshes; similar to the barrier island, except connected to the mainland

Barrier Island -- a coastal insular landform, an island typically between the ocean (or possibly the Great Lakes) and the mainland; its presence usually promotes the formation of salt marshes on the backside

Basin -- a depressional (concave) landform; various types are further defined by the absence of a stream (isolated), by the presence of a stream and its position relative to a wetland (throughflow, outflow, inflow), or by its occurrence on a floodplain (floodplain basins include ox-bows and sloughs, for example)

Bay -- a coastal embayment of variable size and shape that is always opens to the sea through an inlet or other features

Carolina Bay -- a wetland formed in a semicircular or egg-shaped basin with a northwest to southeast orientation, found along the Atlantic Coastal Plain from southern New Jersey to Florida, and perhaps most common in Horry County, South Carolina

Channelization -- the act or result of excavating a stream or river channel to increase downstream flow of water or to increase depth for navigational purposes

Channelized -- water flow through a conspicuous drainageway, a stream or a river

Coastal Island -- an island in marine and estuarine areas

Coastal Pond -- pond and its associated wetlands that form behind a barrier beach and are subjected to varying tidal influence (intermittent to daily); the tidal connection for many coastal ponds has been stabilized by jetties; the ones that are only intermittently connected have low salinities

Connecting Channel -- a river or stream that connects two adjacent lakes; lakes are typically close together considering their relative size; it is not any stream that occurs between two lakes in a drainage basin; perhaps the best examples are rivers connecting the Great Lakes, such as the St. Marys River connecting Lake Superior to Lake Huron, Detroit River connecting Lake St. Clair to Lake Erie, and the Niagara River connecting Lake Erie with Lake Ontario

Cypress Dome -- a wetland dominated by bald cypress growing in a basin that may be formed by the collapse of underlying limestone, forest canopy takes on a domed appearance with tallest trees in center and becoming progressively shorter as move toward margins of basin

Delta -- a typically lobed-shaped or fan-shaped landform formed by sedimentation processes at the mouth of a river carrying heavy sediment loads

Ditch -- a linear, often shallow, artificial channel created by excavation with intent to improve drainage of or to irrigate adjacent lands

Drained, Partly -- condition where a wetland has been ditched or tiled to lower the ground water table, but the area is still wet long enough and often enough to fall within the range of conditions associated with wetland hydrology

Entrenched -- condition where a stream cuts through a wetland and does not periodically overflow into the wetland; the affected wetland may be a terrene wetland cut by a stream or it could be a lotic wetland along an entrenched stream (the latter would usually have to be identified in the field)

Estuarine -- the landscape of estuaries (salt and brackish tidal waterbodies, such as bays and coastal rivers) including associated wetlands, typically occurring in sheltered or protected areas, not exposed to oceanic currents

Flat -- a relatively level landform; may be a component of a floodplain or the landform of an interfluve

Flatwood -- forest of pines, hardwoods or mixed stands growing on interfluves on the Gulf-Atlantic Coastal Plain, typically with imperfectly drained soils; some flatwoods are wetlands, while others are dryland

Floodplain -- a broad, generally flat landform occurring in a landscape shaped by fluvial or riverine processes; for purposes of this classification limited to the broad plain associated with large river systems subject to periodic flooding (once every 100 years) and typically having alluvial soils; further subdivided into several subcategories: flat (broad, nearly level to gently sloping areas) and basin (depressional features such as ox-bows and sloughs)

Floodplain, active -- floodplain that is typically inundated once every 100 years by natural events

Floodplain, inactive -- floodplain that is no longer flooded once in 100 years due to human-alterations such as leveeing, diking, or altered river flow regimes or to natural processes such as changing river courses

Fringe -- a wetland occurring along a standing or flowing waterbody, i.e., a lake, pond, river, stream, estuary, or ocean, including tidal wetlands that are inundated frequently by tides, nontidal vegetated wetlands that are flooded for most of the growing season, and nonvegetated wetlands that form the banks of these waterbodies (such as cobble-gravel bars along river bends)

Ground Water -- water below ground, held in the soil or underground aquifers

Headland -- the seaward edge of the major continental land mass (North America), commonly called the mainland; not an island

High Gradient -- the fast-flowing segment of a drainage system, typically with no floodplain development; equivalent to the Upper Perennial and Intermittent Subsystems of the Riverine System in Cowardin et al. 1979

Inflow -- water enters; an inflow wetland is one that receives surface water from a stream or other waterbody or from significant surface or ground water from a wetland or waterbody at a higher elevation and has no significant discharge

Interdunal -- occurring between sand dunes, as in interdunal swale wetlands found in dunefields behind ocean and estuarine beaches and in sand plains like the Nebraska Sandhills

Interfluve -- a broad level to imperceptibly depressional poorly drained landform occurring between two drainage systems, most typical of the Coastal Plain

Island -- a landform completely surrounded by water and not a delta; some islands are entirely wetland, while others are uplands with or without a fringe wetland

Isolated -- lacking an apparent surface water connection to other wetlands and waterbodies; typically "geographically isolated" (surrounded by upland - nonhydric soils); may be connected to other wetlands and water via groundwater, but this is not known

Karst -- a limestone region characterized by sinkholes and underground caverns

Kettle -- a glacially formed depression typically created by a block of glacial ice left on the land by a retreating glacier; melting of the ice formed a kettle pond that may be quite deep, with bog vegetation frequently established along its perimeter

Lake Island -- an island in a lake

Lentic -- the landscape position associated with large, deep standing waterbodies (such as lakes and reservoirs) and contiguous wetlands formed in the lake basin (excludes seasonal and shallow lakes which are included in the *Terrene* landscape position)

Lotic -- the landscape position associated with flowing water systems (such as rivers, creeks, perennial streams, intermittent streams, and similar waterbodies) and contiguous wetlands

Low Gradient -- the slow-flowing segment of a drainage system, typically with considerable floodplain development; equivalent to the Lower Perennial Subsystem of the Riverine System in Cowardin et al. 1979 plus contiguous wetlands

Marine -- the landscape position (or seascape) associated with the ocean's shoreline

Middle Gradient -- the segment of a drainage system with characteristic intermediate between the high and low gradient reaches, typically with limited floodplain development; equivalent to areas mapped as Riverine Unknown (R5) in the Northeast Region plus contiguous wetlands

Nonchannelized -- water exits through seepage, not through a river or stream channel or ditch

Outflow -- water exits naturally or through artificial means (e.g., ditches); an outflow wetland has water leaving via a stream, seepage, or ditch (artificial) to a wetland or waterbody at a lower elevation; it lacks an inflowing surface water source like an intermittent or perennial stream

Oxbow -- a former mainstem river bend now partly or completely cut off from mainstem

Paludified -- subjected to paludification, the process by which peat moss engulfs terrains of varying elevations due to an excess of water, typically associated with cold, humid climates of northern areas (boreal/arctic regions and fog-shrouded coasts)

Playa -- a type of basin wetland in the Southwest characterized by drastic fluctuations in water levels over the normal wet-dry cycle

Pocosin -- a shrub and/or forested wetland forming on organic soils in interstream divides (interfluves) on the Atlantic Coast Plain from Virginia to Florida, mostly in North Carolina

Pond -- a natural or human-made shallow open waterbody that may be subjected to periodic drawdowns

Prairie Pothole -- a glacially formed basin wetland found in the Upper Midwest especially in the Dakotas, western Minnesota, and Iowa

Reservoir -- a large, deep waterbody formed by a dike or dam created for a water supply for drinking water or agricultural purposes or for flood control, or similar purposes

River Island -- an island within a river

Salt Pond -- a coastal embayment of variable size and shape that is periodically and temporarily cut off from the sea by natural accretion processes; some may be kept permanently open by jetties and periodic maintenance dredging

Salt Flat -- a broad expanse of alkaline wetlands associated with arid regions, especially the Great Basin in the western United States

Sinkhole -- a depression formed by the collapse of underlying limestone deposits; may be wetland or nonwetland depending on drainage characteristics

Slope -- a wetland occurring on a slope; various types include those along a sloping stream (fringe), those (paludified) formed by paludification -- the process of bogging or swamping of uplands by peat moss in northern climes (humid and cold), and those not designated as one of the above and typically called seeps

Stream -- a natural drainageway that contains flowing water at least seasonally; different stream types: *perennial* where water flows continously in all years except drought or extremely dry years; <u>intermittent</u> where water flows only seasonally in most years; <u>channelized</u> where stream bed has been excavated or dredged

Subsurface Flow -- water leaves via ground water

Surface Water -- water occurring above the ground as in flooded or ponded conditions

Tectonic -- changes in the earth's surface caused by landslides, faulting, and volcanic activity

Terrene -- wetlands surrounded or nearly so by uplands and lacking a channelized outlet stream; a stream may enter or exit this type of wetland but it does not flow through it as a channel; includes a variety of wetlands and natural and human-made ponds

Throughflow -- water entering and exiting, passing through; a throughflow wetland receives significant surface or ground water which passes through the wetland and is discharged to a stream, wetland or other waterbody at a lower elevation; throughflow may be perennial, intermittent, or associated with an entrenched stream

Tidal Gradient -- the segment of a drainage basin that is subjected to tidal influence; essentially the freshwater tidal reach of coastal rivers; equivalent to the Tidal Subsystem of the Riverine System in Cowardin et al. 1979 plus contiguous wetlands

Vernal Pool -- a temporarily flooded basin; woodland vernal pools are found in humid temperature regions dominated by trees, these pools are surrounded by upland forests, are usually flooded from winter through mid-summer, and serve as critical breeding grounds for salamanders and woodland frogs; West Coast vernal pools occur in California, Oregon, and Washington on clayey soils, they are important habitats for many rare plants and animals

www.ingramcontent.com/pod-product-compliance
Lightning Source LLC
Chambersburg PA
CBHW080617290526
45790CB00007B/2816